W9-BYB-244

Primary Sources

Leia Tait

WEIGL PUBLISHERS INC.

Published by Weigl Publishers Inc.
350 5th Avenue, Suite 3304, PMB 6G
New York, NY 10118-0069

Website: www.weigl.com

Copyright ©2008 WEIGL PUBLISHERS INC.
All rights reserved. No part of this publication may be reproduced, stored in a retrieval system, or transmitted in any form or by any means, electronic, mechanical, photocopying, recording, or otherwise, without the prior written permission of the publisher.

All of the Internet URLs given in the book were valid at the time of publication. However, due to the dynamic nature of the Internet, some addresses may have changed, or sites may have ceased to exist since publication. While the author and publisher regret any inconvenience this may cause readers, no responsibility for any such changes can be accepted by either the author or the publisher.

Library of Congress Cataloging-in-Publication Data

Tait, Leia.
  Primary sources / Leia Tait.
    p. cm. -- (Social studies essential skills)
  Includes index.
  ISBN 978-1-59036-763-6 (library binding : alk. paper) -- ISBN 978-1-59036-764-3 (soft cover : alk. paper)
  1. Information resources--Juvenile literature. 2. History--Sources--Juvenile literature. 3. United States--History--Sources--Juvenile literature. I. Title.
  ZA3070.T35 2008
  020--dc22
                              2007024014

Printed in the United States of America
1 2 3 4 5 6 7 8 9 0 11 10 09 08 07

Editor: Heather C. Hudak
Design: Terry Paulhus

Every reasonable effort has been made to trace ownership and to obtain permission to reprint copyright material. The publishers would be pleased to have any errors or omissions brought to their attention so that they may be corrected in subsequent printings.

Table of Contents

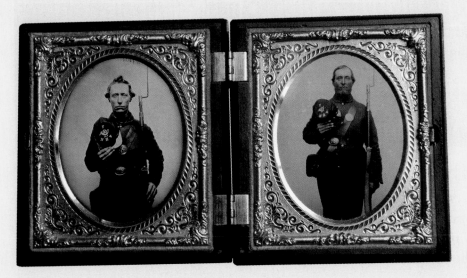

99 093

What is a Primary Source?

A primary source is a document or record that provides a firsthand account of an event, a time period, or a particular subject. Primary sources are created at the time an event occurs. They are made by individuals who witness or participate in the event. Primary sources are the first **evidence** of something happening.

Letters, diaries, and similar documents are primary sources because they provide a firsthand account of events in a person's life. Photographs are also primary sources, as are newspaper articles, maps, school records, and speeches. Each of these items is a record of events. They can be used to reconstruct a person's life, or the events that took place around him or her.

Primary sources, such as photographs, can be used to answer questions. Think about how the U.S. president travels from place to place. Now, look at the picture above. How does this image help you answer your question? What information is missing? What else can you learn about the president from this image?

Primary Sources In Your Life

We create and use primary sources every day. They may be notes, letters, or emails. Look at the pictures of some primary sources that you make or use every day. Make a list of the items in your notebook. Beside each item, write what it reveals about you. What would the item tell someone who does not know you? Then, make a list of some other primary sources that you create each day.

Drawings or doodles

Friendly notes

Postcards

Calendar

Homework

A Diary

Movie or concert tickets

Music sheets

Email messages

Official documents

Primary or Secondary?

Most often, primary sources are used to learn about history. **Historians** study primary sources to discover the beliefs, values, opinions, experiences, and **traditions** of people from the past. They use this information to create secondary sources. Secondary sources are secondhand accounts. They are made by people not directly involved in the events or time period they are addressing. Secondary sources express an opinion or an argument about past events. Textbooks, **research** articles, and biographies are examples of secondary sources.

Some records can be used as both primary and secondary sources. A painting of Christopher Columbus made in the 1800s can be used as a secondary source about him today. The same painting can also be used as a primary source about the 1800s. It can reveal how the artist living then might have felt about Columbus and his discovery of the Americas.

Compare the portrait on the left, created around 1500, to that on the right, made in the 1800s. How did people in these years imagine Columbus differently?

SOCIAL STUDIES ESSENTIAL SKILLS

Compare Primary and Secondary Sources

Read the paragraphs below about the first Thanksgiving. Which paragraph is a primary source? Which is a secondary source? Think about how the sources are different. What you have learned from each source? Why do you think historians use both primary and secondary sources when studying history?

I) *The governor sent four men hunting, so that we might rejoice together in a special way after we had gathered the fruits of our labor. In one day, these four men killed enough fowl to serve the company almost a week. During that time, many of the Indians came among us. For three days, we celebrated and feasted together. The Indians killed deer, which they gave to the governor, the captain, and others.*

II) *The pilgrims arrived in Plymouth, Massachusetts, in the winter of 1620. They had very little food to eat. The Wampanoag Indians taught them how to farm the new land and build houses. The* **colony** *may not have survived without the Indians' help. By the next autumn, the pilgrims had food to eat and homes to live in. They celebrated with a harvest festival. They invited the Indians to join them. The feast lasted three days.*

Understanding Context

Some primary sources cannot be understood without knowing their context. Context is the set of facts or circumstances that surround a situation or event. By knowing a source's context, readers can determine its meaning.

To determine the context of a source, it is important to ask questions. Who created the source? What was his or her profession? When and where did he or she create the source? What was happening at that time and place? Doing research can help readers answer these questions. This means going to the library to read books on the topic or searching the Internet for additional information.

Without knowing the context of this painting, what can you determine about the event shown? How would your understanding change if you learned that the event happened in Salem, Massachusetts, in the late 1600s?

Mapping the Past

This map shows the British colonies in North America as they looked in 1763. It is titled "A Map of the British Dominions in North America, according to the Treaty in 1763; by Peter Bell, Geographer, 1772."

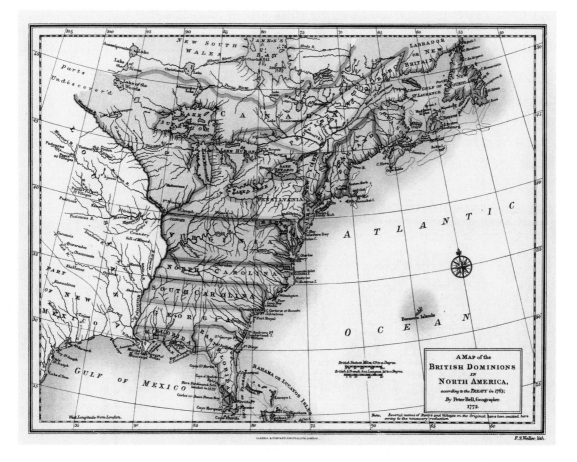

Use the details included in the map to determine its context. For example, the map was created in 1772. Why might the mapmaker have chosen to show the land as it looked in 1763? Was there an important event that happened that year? To find out, do some research at **http://www.ohiohistorycentral.org/ entry.php?rec=1857**. Read the title of the map again. What treaty does the map's title refer to? Now, think about the mapmaker. What is his profession? Do you feel the same about this map as you would about one created by a farmer? Why? Continue to examine the map. What other things can you learn?

Working with Purpose

All primary sources have a purpose or reason why they were created. Different types of sources have different purposes. A diary may be written to record a person's private thoughts. Government documents might be used to create laws. Photos may be taken to **preserve** memories of things, or they might be created as art. Other sources, such as posters or speeches, might be intended to **persuade** people into acting or thinking a certain way.

You can use a source's context to help determine its purpose. First, research when the source was created. Then, ask what events, issues, or problems it was addressing. Was the person who created it trying to make a certain point? What result did he or she expect?

This cartoon was first published in a newspaper by politician Benjamin Franklin in 1754. It referred to the unfriendliness that existed between the colonies at that time. What was its purpose? What result do you think Franklin was hoping for when he published the cartoon?

Recognizing Purpose

Read the historical passages below. Use clues in the text to determine the purpose of each source. Then, compare the documents. How are they different? How do these differences relate to each document's purpose? What are the similarities?

The Declaration of Independence (1776)

When in the Course of human events, it becomes necessary for one people to dissolve the political bands which have connected them with another, and to assume among the powers of the earth, the separate and equal station to which the Laws of Nature and of Nature's God entitle them, a decent respect to the opinions of mankind requires that they should declare the causes which impel them to the separation.

Learn more about the Declaration of Independence at **www.congressforkids.net/ Independence_declaration_1.htm**.

The Star Spangled Banner (1814)

*O! say can you see by the dawn's early light
What so proudly we hail'd at the twilight's
last gleaming,
Whose broad stripes and bright stars,
through the perilous fight
O'er the ramparts we watch'd were
so gallantly streaming?
And the Rockets red glare, the Bombs bursting in air,
Gave proof through the night that our
Flag was still there!*

To learn about the Star Spangled Banner, visit **http://americanhistory.si.edu/ssb**.

Finding an Audience

Every primary source is created for an audience. This means the source is meant to be used or viewed by a specific person or group of people. For example, a diary is usually meant to be read only by its author. Letters are meant for the people they are addressed to. Speeches are written for those attending a specific event. Newspapers are read by members of a certain community.

Knowing the audience of a source can help you better understand its purpose. The source can tell you what the author thought about the audience. To discover the audience of a source, ask yourself some key questions. Is the source addressed to anyone? Does it refer to an event in a particular community? What kind of language is used? If it is formal, the source may be intended for a professional audience. If it is simple, it may be meant for young people. Think about the source's purpose. If the source is meant to persuade someone, who is it?

This illustration appeared in a fashion advertisement in 1868. Who is the audience? How can you tell?

Recognizing Audience

This brief story appeared in a book around 1850. Read the story. Who is the audience? How can you tell?

The Peacock

Did you ever see a Peacock? He seems very proud of his beautiful feathers. He often spreads his tail like a fan, and struts about as though he wanted people to notice his fine dress; and don't you think that pride looks very foolish? But I have sometimes seen little children who seemed quite as proud as the poor, silly peacock. I have seen a little girl with a fine new dress, and a little boy with a fine new jacket, who were so proud of their clothes that they thought everybody was admiring them; and they could think of nothing else. Now we all like to have good clothes, and it is right we should; but it isn't our clothes that makes us good. I have seen a little girl dressed very nicely, who was very cross; and do you think any one liked her any better because she wore a silk dress? Everybody loves good boys and girls, whatever may be their dress.

What is Bias?

Primary sources reflect the values, opinions, and feelings of the people who create them. As a result, they contain bias. Bias is a preference or attitude that causes individuals to unfairly judge people or events in the world around them.

All primary sources have some bias. This is because they present only one version of events—that of the person who created the source. Some bias can be helpful. It shows what people in the past thought about certain topics. Sources that are too one-sided, however, can cause readers to forget that there may be other ways to explain events.

To identify bias in primary sources, consult more than one source per topic. Information that is supported by multiple sources is usually factual. Information that only appears in one source may be a matter of opinion or a mistake.

Look at the painting. It shows the death of well-known American Indian leader Tecumseh, in 1813. What biases does the creator of this painting reveal? How do you think he feels about Tecumseh?

Identifying Bias in Primary Sources

Read the following excerpt from a letter about New York City. It was written by Mark Twain on June 5, 1867. How does the author feel about New York City? How can you tell? In your notebook, list the author's opinions. Review the list of opinions. What bias do they show?

There is something about this ceaseless buzz, and hurry, and bustle, that keeps a stranger in a state of unwholesome excitement all the time, and makes him restless and uneasy, and saps from him all capacity to enjoy anything or take a strong interest in any matter whatever—a something which impels him to try to do everything, and yet permits him to do nothing. He is a boy in a candy-shop—could choose quickly if there were but one kind of candy, but is hopelessly undetermined in the midst of a hundred kinds. A stranger feels unsatisfied, here, a good part of the time.

Personal Bias

People who read or study primary sources may have a bias. This is called a personal bias. Just as individuals might explain the same event differently, they might **interpret** a document or photograph in different ways. A person's interpretation of a primary source is shaped by his or her own values, opinions, and experiences. As a result, the information may be biased.

When judging a primary source, be aware of your own personal bias. If you dislike broccoli, you may not agree with a source that recommends eating it. This would be unfair, especially if the author provided evidence to support his or her claim.

In the past, words and phrases that are not used today may have been commonplace. Always judge a source by the standards of the time when it was created, not by those in place today.

Describe the car in this photo. If you used words like "old," "simple," or "slow," you are judging the car by today's standards. To avoid this kind of personal bias, think about how the car would have been described in 1900.

What If You Were There?

Imagining what life was like when a primary source was made can help you avoid having a personal bias about it.

Visit **www.history.com/ minisites/ellisisland**, and learn about the history of U.S. **immigration**. Read the accounts written by immigrants, and look at the photographs. Then, imagine you were at Ellis Island waiting to enter the United States as an immigrant. Write a letter to your friends and family back home describing the experience. What was your journey to Ellis Island like? What happened when you arrived there? What did you do to pass your time while you were waiting? What emotions are you experiencing? What will you do when you are finally allowed to enter the United States?

Evaluating Primary Sources

Some primary sources are better than others. To evaluate the strengths and weaknesses of a primary source, ask yourself these questions. Does this source help you answer questions about the topic? What questions does it answer? What new questions does it create? Does the source fit with others from the same time period or about the same topic?

The best sources are those that are credible, or trustworthy. Credible sources are created by someone with firsthand knowledge of the subject. Facts in these sources can be confirmed with information from other accounts. Sources that display a strong bias are not credible. To be sure a source is credible, ask yourself if it was created by someone with firsthand knowledge of the topic. Is the source based more on fact than opinion? Has the author made any factual mistakes? Does he or she have a reason to avoid being truthful?

"SUB SPOTTED—
LET 'EM HAVE IT!"

LEND A HAND – Enlist in your Navy today

Look at the poster. It was used during World War I to encourage people to join the U.S. Navy. Is it a good source to learn about the experiences of men fighting in the navy at that time?

Comparing Credibility

Look at the two images below. Both were created during the **Great Depression**. The billboard was paid for by the National Association of Manufacturers in 1937. The photograph below was taken in 1938. Which image is more credible? Which one would be a better source of information about the Great Depression? Why?

Forming Conclusions

You can use your knowledge of context, purpose, audience, bias, and credibility to interpret primary sources and form your own conclusions about the events of the past.

An important part of working with primary sources is presenting your findings. Most historians present their findings in essays or papers. You can write a short essay to present your findings. Begin your essay by stating what you believed happened. Offer facts to support your view. Facts provide reasons for readers to agree with you. Include facts from more than one source. You can use your interpretation of these facts to **debate** explanations made by others and to challenge their conclusions. End your essay with a strong statement that supports your view on what you think happened. Your essay could then be used as a secondary source.

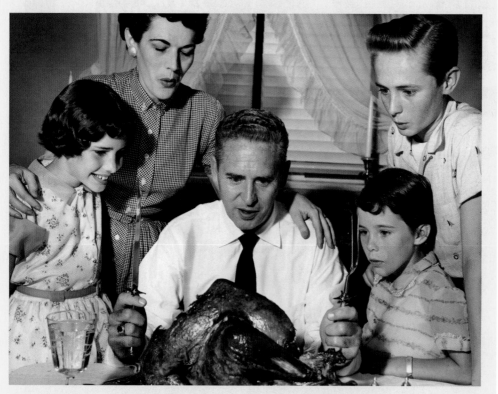

Based on this photo, what conclusions can you make about life in the 1950s?

Creating Secondary Sources

Use the primary sources below to answer the question, "Why was Rosa Parks arrested?" Remember to consider the context, purpose, and audience of each source. Look for bias in the sources, and be aware of your own attitudes towards them. Then, write a short essay presenting your findings about Rosa's arrest. Why was she arrested? Who was in the wrong? Was this event part of a larger problem?

I) Chapter 6, Section 11 Montgomery City Code
Any employee in charge of a bus operated in the city shall have the powers of a police officer of the city while in actual charge of any bus....and it shall be unlawful for any passenger to refuse or fail to take a seat among those assigned to the race to which he belongs, at the request of any such employee in charge, if there is such a seat vacant.

II)

III) Warrant #14254 (December 1, 1955)
The bus operator said he had a coloured female sitting in the white section of the bus, and would not move back. We (officers Day and Mixon) also saw her. The bus operator signed a warrant for her. Rosa Parks (cf), 634 Cleveland Court. Rosa Parks (cf) was charged with violating chapter 6, section 11 of the Montgomery City Code.

Put Your Knowledge to Use

Put your knowledge of primary sources to use by creating a time capsule. Time capsules are used to teach people in the future about life today.

Find a cardboard box or plastic container with a lid. This will be your time capsule. Begin by writing a letter to someone in the future. In the letter, describe yourself, your home, your school, and your community. Include any other information you think would be useful to someone in the future. When you are done, set your letter aside. It will be the last thing you put in your time capsule.

Now, choose other primary sources to put in your time capsule. These can be photographs, drawings, objects, or other documents. Make a list of these items in your notebook. Beside each item, explain what it could teach someone from the future about life today. Identify the context, purpose, and audience of each item, along with any biases. Once you have filled your time capsule, add your letter as the last item. Then, seal the lid. Decorate and label the box so that others will know it is a time capsule. Put it somewhere safe to be opened at a later date.

Websites for Further Research

Primary sources can be found in many places. Official records, such as **census** figures and court reports, can be found in government offices. Public libraries or archives often keep copies of old newspapers and magazines. Photographs, maps, and works of art can be found in **archives**. Museums and historical organizations are other excellent places to start your search.

Many books and websites provide information on working with primary sources. To learn more about using primary sources, type key words, such as "primary sources," into the search field of your Web browser. There are many sites that teach about American history. You can visit these sites to practice using primary sources.

Visit *The Learning Page* to take a workshop about primary sources and how to use them. http://memory.loc.gov/learn/start/prim_sources.html

America's Library, at www.americaslibrary.gov, provides fun facts, exciting puzzles, and intriguing primary sources.

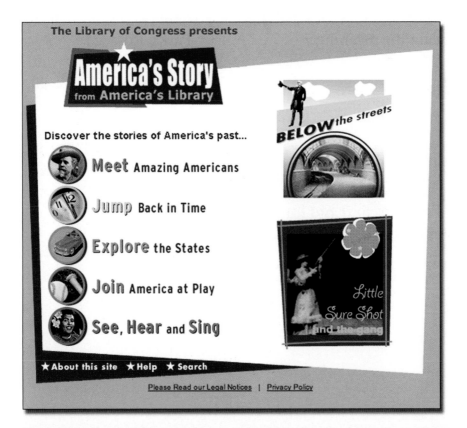

Glossary

archives: places in which public records or historical documents are kept

census: a government's counting of the population of a country, city, or town, and gathering of related information

colony: a group of people sent by a state to settle a new territory

debate: a formal discussion presenting more than one argument

evidence: proof of something

Great Depression: a time during the 1930s when the economy was so poor that many people were unemployed

historians: people who study the past

immigration: the act of coming to live in a new country

interpret: to explain the meaning of something

persuade: to cause someone to think or do something through reasoning or arguing

preserve: protect from injury, loss, or ruin

research: careful study to find and learn facts, and to explain new knowledge

traditions: information, beliefs, or customs handed down from one generation to another

Index

EAST SMITHFIELD PUBLIC LIBRARY

3 2895 00105 2021